First Facts™

Holidays and Culture

Chinese New Year

Festival of New Beginnings

by Terri Sievert

Consultant:
Richard Gunde
Assistant Director
UCLA Center for Chinese Studies
Los Angeles, California

Capstone press

Mankato, Minnesota

First Facts is published by Capstone Press,
151 Good Counsel Drive, P.O. Box 669, Mankato, Minnesota 56002.
www.capstonepress.com

Library of Congress Cataloging-in-Publication Data
Sievert, Terri.
    Chinese New Year : festival of new beginnings/by Terri Sievert.
    p. cm.—(First facts. Holidays and culture)
    Summary: "A brief description of what Chinese New Year is, how it started, and ways people
celebrate this cultural holiday"—Provided by publisher.
    Includes bibliographical references and index.
    ISBN-13: 978-0-7368-5386-6 (hardcover)
    ISBN-10: 0-7368-5386-3 (hardcover)
    1. Chinese New Year—Juvenile literature. I. Title. II. Series.
GT4905.S54 2006
394.261—dc22   2005015586

Editorial Credits
Jennifer Besel, editor; Juliette Peters, designer; Wanda Winch, photo researcher; Scott Thoms,
    photo editor

Photo Credits
Capstone Press/Karon Dubke, 12, 13, 18–19, 21
Corbis/Morton Beebe, 20; Nik Wheeler, 7; Phil Schermeister, 10, 11, 14; Reuters/Jason Lee, 6;
    XINHUA/Ding Xiaochun, cover
Folio, Inc./Evan Sheppard, 9
iStockphoto/Ulrike Hammerich, 1
Photri-MicroStock/L. Balterman, 4–5
Special Collections, Yale Divinity School Library, 17
SuperStock Inc./Superstock, 15

1 2 3 4 5 6 11 10 09 08 07 06

Table of Contents

Celebrating Chinese New Year

A colorful paper dragon slithers down the street. As it passes, firecrackers pop to scare away evil and bad luck. On this day, it's important to avoid bad luck. It's the Chinese New Year, and bad luck today could mean bad luck all year!

Fact!

For 15 days, the Chinese celebrate the start of the new year. They wish for good luck in the months ahead.

5

What Is Chinese New Year?

Chinese New Year is the start of a new **lunar** year. In China, people use a calendar that follows the movements of the moon. The lunar year doesn't start on January 1. It begins between January 21 and February 19.

Chinese Americans celebrate their
culture at the beginning of each lunar
year. They honor their **heritage** and
celebrate their way of life.

A Monster

Chinese New Year traditions began thousands of years ago as a way to scare a monster. A **legend** says a monster called Nian (nee-UHN) attacked the Chinese people.

Nian was afraid of noise, light, and the color red. So the people built fires, hung red signs, and lit firecrackers. Today, similar **customs** are part of new year celebrations.

Fact!
The word *nian* means year in Chinese.

Good Luck

No one wants to start the new year out on the wrong foot. Many new year traditions are meant to bring good luck. Children are given money in red *hongbao* (HONG-bou) envelopes to bring them wealth in the new year.

Families also buy flowers before the new year, hoping they will bloom. A blooming flower on New Year's Day is a sign of good luck and long life.

Getting Ready

Before the new year arrives, families sweep their houses clean. Then they put the broom away. Sweeping on New Year's Day could sweep away good luck.

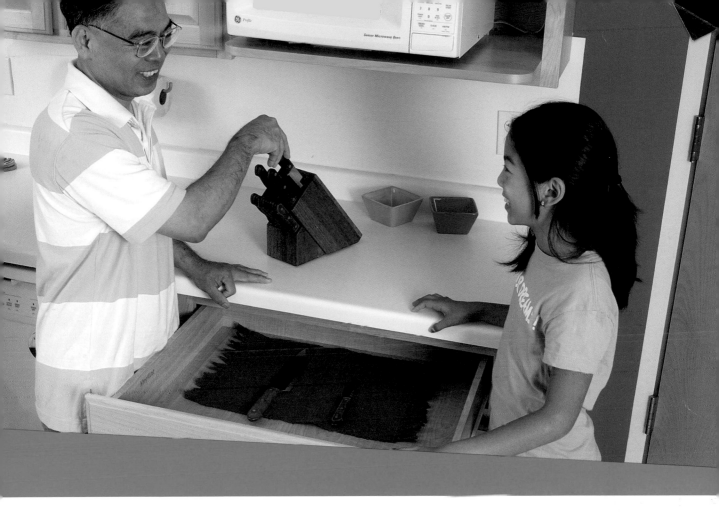

Another new year's custom is to put all the knives away. Families don't want to cut off their good luck. So they make all their holiday food before New Year's Day.

New Year's Eve

Sitting around a table full of their favorite Chinese dishes makes families excited for a new year. *Nian gao* (nee-UHN GO), or year cakes, sweeten the celebration.

At midnight, fireworks welcome the new year. The loud noises and lights remind families of the Nian monster legend and their Chinese heritage.

The Kitchen God

Almost every Chinese family has a picture of the kitchen god in their home. According to custom, the kitchen god watches the family all year. At year's end, the family burns his picture, returning him to the spirit world. There, he reports on the family's behavior. On New Year's Day, the family hangs a new picture of the kitchen god to welcome him back.

Fact!

Paper money is burned with the kitchen god's picture to pay for his trip.

The kitchen god, right, and his wife

18

Altars

In Chinese culture, it is very important to honor relatives. For the new year, families decorate **altars** with pictures and food to honor family members who have died. These altars remind families of their past, even as they look forward to the future.

Amazing Holiday Story!

In the 1860s, many Chinese people moved to San Francisco to find work. Many of the people missed the customs of their homeland. They decided to hold a parade to celebrate the Chinese New Year. They marched with bright flags and colorful signs. Firecrackers popped and flared.

Today, San Francisco holds the largest Chinese New Year celebration in the United States. Thousands of people come to see the parade every year.

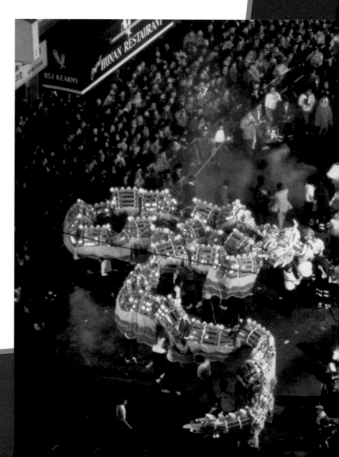

Hands On: Chinese Dragon

Chinese dragons are thought to bring good luck. You can make a dragon to use in your own Chinese New Year parade.

What You Need

large brown paper bag
scissors
markers
construction paper
glue
crepe paper

What You Do

1. Open the paper bag. Cut two holes where you want the eyes.
2. Use the markers, construction paper, glue, and crepe paper to decorate your Chinese dragon. Give your dragon a face, complete with teeth, a red tongue, and colored eyes. Use the crepe paper to give your dragon a beard or hair.
3. Your dragon is ready for the Chinese New Year parade.

Glossary

altar (AWL-tur)—a table used for religious ceremonies or rituals

culture (KUHL-chur)—a people's way of life, ideas, art, customs, and traditions

custom (KUHSS-tuhm)—a tradition in a culture or society

heritage (HER-uh-tij)—history and traditions handed down from the past

legend (LEJ-uhnd)—a story handed down from earlier times; legends are often based on fact, but they are not entirely true.

lunar (LOO-nur)—having to do with the moon; China uses a lunar calendar that follows the cycles of the moon around the earth.

Read More

Flanagan, Alice K. *Chinese New Year.* Holidays and Festivals. Minneapolis: Compass Point Books, 2004.

Kaplan, Leslie C. *Chinese New Year.* The Library of Holidays. New York: PowerKids Press, 2004.

Internet Sites

FactHound offers a safe, fun way to find Internet sites related to this book. All of the sites on FactHound have been researched by our staff.

Here's how:
1. Visit *www.facthound.com*
2. Type in this special code **0736853863** for age-appropriate sites. Or enter a search word related to this book for a more general search.
3. Click on the **Fetch It** button.

FactHound will fetch the best sites for you!

Index